THIS BOOK BELONGS TO:

CONTACT INFORMATION	
NAME:	
ADDRESS:	
PHONE:	

START / END DATES

___ / ___ / ___   TO   ___ / ___ / ___

DEDICATION

This Baby's Daily Log Journal is dedicated to all the parents out there who want to track their baby's daily schedule and document their findings in the process.

You are my inspiration for producing books and I'm honored to be a part of keeping all of your baby's notes and records organized.

This journal notebook will help you record your details about your baby's schedule and memorable moments.

Thoughtfully put together with these sections to record:

Baby's Information, Memorable Moments, Growth, Immunization Record, Feeding Schedule, Temperature Readings, Diaper Changes, Nap Time, Food, Reminders, Doctors Appointments/ Medical, Medicine Tracker Notes and more!

HOW TO USE THIS BOOK

The purpose of this book is to keep all of your baby's notes all in one place. It will help keep you organized.

This Baby's Daily Log Journal will allow you to accurately document every detail about your precious little baby. It's a great way to chart your course through recording everything about your baby.

Here are examples of the prompts for you to fill in and write about your experience in this book:

1. **Baby's Information** - Name, Birthday, Sex, Blood Type, Birth Weight & Length, Head & Chest Circumference, Parents Names, Pediatrician's Info, Allergies

2. **Memorable Moments** - First Day Home From Hospital, 1st Smile, 1st Roll, 1st Crawl, 1st Tooth, 1st Stand, 1st Step, 1st Solid Food, 1st Family Outing, Said Mama & Dada, Slept Through The Night, etc.

3. **Growth** - Age, Weight & Height For Months 0-12.

4. **Immunization Record** - Vaccine, Date, Dose, Notes.

5. **Feeding Schedule** - Date, Time, Breastfeeding/ Bottle, Duration, Amount, Feedings Notes & Schedules.

6. **Temperature Readings** - Date, Method, Temp, Notes.

7. **Diaper Changes** - Time, Pee, or Poop.

8. **Nap Time** - Start Time, Wake Up Time, Total Time.

9. **Food** - Time, Food, Amount.

10. **Reminders** - Any important information you want to write.

11. **Doctors Appointments/ Medical** - Date, Doctor, Reason/ Diagnosis, Medicine.

12. **Medicine Tracker Notes** - Medication Name, Dosage, Times Per Day, Date, Time Given, Next Due, Remarks.

13. **Additional Notes** - Blank lined for any important information you want, any advice you received, best practices, etc.

BABY'S INFORMATION

BABY'S PERSONAL INFORMATION

NAME:		
BIRTHDAY:	SEX:	BLOOD TYPE:
BIRTH WEIGHT:	BIRTH LENGTH:	
HEAD CIRCUMFERENCE:	CHEST CIRCUMFERENCE:	

PARENT'S INFORMATION

MOTHER'S NAME:
FATHER'S NAME:

PEDIATRICIAN'S INFORMATION

NAME:
ADDRESS:
CONTACT NUMBER:

ALLERGIES

MEMORABLE MOMENTS

EVENT	DATE	NOTES
FIRST DAY HOME FROM HOSPITAL		
FIRST SMILE		
FIRST ROLL		
FIRST CRAWL		
FIRST TOOTH		
FIRST STAND		
FIRST STEP		
FIRST SOLID FOOD		
FIRST FAMILY OUTING		
SAID MAMA AND DADA		
SLEPT THROUGH THE NIGHT		
SAT UP, ROLLED OVER, CRAWLED		
FIRST LAUGH		

BABY'S GROWTH

(FOR 0 - 12 MONTHS)

AGE	WEIGHT (KG)	HEIGHT (CM)
NEWBORN		
1 MONTH		
2 MONTHS		
3 MONTHS		
4 MONTHS		
5 MONTHS		
6 MONTHS		
7 MONTHS		
8 MONTHS		
9 MONTHS		
10 MONTHS		
11 MONTHS		
12 MONTHS		

IMMUNIZATION RECORD

VACCINE	DATE	DOSE	NOTES

FEEDING SCHEDULE

DATE:

TIME	DURATION (BREASTFEEDING)	AMOUNT (BOTTLE)	NOTES

DIAPER

TIME	PEE	POOP

NAP TIME

START TIME	WAKEUP TIME	TOTAL MINUTES/ HOURS

FOOD

TIME	FOOD	AMOUNT

NOTES & REMINDERS

BABY'S TEMPERATURE

METHOD	RANGE
RECTUM	97.9 °F TO 100.4 °F
MOUTH	95.9 °F TO 99.5 °F
ARMPIT	97.8 °F TO 99.5 °F
EAR	96.4 °F TO 100.4 °F

DATE	TEMPERATURE	NOTES

DOCTOR'S APPOINTMENT

DATE	DOCTOR	REASON / DIAGNOSIS	MEDICATION

MEDICINE TRACKING

MEDICATION NAME:

DOSAGE: TIMES PER DAY:

DATE	TIME GIVEN	NEXT DUE	REMARKS

ADDITIONAL NOTES

FEEDING SCHEDULE

DATE:

TIME	DURATION (BREASTFEEDING)	AMOUNT (BOTTLE)	NOTES

DIAPER

TIME	PEE	POOP

NAP TIME

START TIME	WAKEUP TIME	TOTAL MINUTES/ HOURS

FOOD

TIME	FOOD	AMOUNT

NOTES & REMINDERS

BABY'S TEMPERATURE

METHOD	RANGE
RECTUM	97.9 °F TO 100.4 °F
MOUTH	95.9 °F TO 99.5 °F
ARMPIT	97.8 °F TO 99.5 °F
EAR	96.4 °F TO 100.4 °F

DATE	TEMPERATURE	NOTES

DOCTOR'S APPOINTMENT

DATE	DOCTOR	REASON / DIAGNOSIS	MEDICATION

MEDICINE TRACKING

MEDICATION NAME:

DOSAGE: TIMES PER DAY:

DATE	TIME GIVEN	NEXT DUE	REMARKS

ADDITIONAL NOTES

FEEDING SCHEDULE

DATE:

TIME	DURATION (BREASTFEEDING)	AMOUNT (BOTTLE)	NOTES

DIAPER

TIME	PEE	POOP

NAP TIME

START TIME	WAKEUP TIME	TOTAL MINUTES/ HOURS

FOOD

TIME	FOOD	AMOUNT

NOTES & REMINDERS

BABY'S TEMPERATURE

METHOD	RANGE
RECTUM	97.9 °F TO 100.4 °F
MOUTH	95.9 °F TO 99.5 °F
ARMPIT	97.8 °F TO 99.5 °F
EAR	96.4 °F TO 100.4 °F

DATE	TEMPERATURE	NOTES

DOCTOR'S APPOINTMENT

DATE	DOCTOR	REASON / DIAGNOSIS	MEDICATION

MEDICINE TRACKING

MEDICATION NAME: _____

DOSAGE: _____   TIMES PER DAY: _____

DATE	TIME GIVEN	NEXT DUE	REMARKS

ADDITIONAL NOTES

FEEDING SCHEDULE

DATE:

TIME	DURATION (BREASTFEEDING)	AMOUNT (BOTTLE)	NOTES

DIAPER

TIME	PEE	POOP

NAP TIME

START TIME	WAKEUP TIME	TOTAL MINUTES/ HOURS

FOOD

TIME	FOOD	AMOUNT

NOTES & REMINDERS

BABY'S TEMPERATURE

METHOD	RANGE
RECTUM	97.9 °F TO 100.4 °F
MOUTH	95.9 °F TO 99.5 °F
ARMPIT	97.8 °F TO 99.5 °F
EAR	96.4 °F TO 100.4 °F

DATE	TEMPERATURE	NOTES

DOCTOR'S APPOINTMENT

DATE	DOCTOR	REASON / DIAGNOSIS	MEDICATION

MEDICINE TRACKING

MEDICATION NAME:

DOSAGE: TIMES PER DAY:

DATE	TIME GIVEN	NEXT DUE	REMARKS

ADDITIONAL NOTES

FEEDING SCHEDULE

DATE:

TIME	DURATION (BREASTFEEDING)	AMOUNT (BOTTLE)	NOTES

DIAPER

TIME	PEE	POOP

NAP TIME

START TIME	WAKEUP TIME	TOTAL MINUTES/ HOURS

FOOD

TIME	FOOD	AMOUNT

NOTES & REMINDERS

BABY'S TEMPERATURE

METHOD	RANGE
RECTUM	97.9 °F TO 100.4 °F
MOUTH	95.9 °F TO 99.5 °F
ARMPIT	97.8 °F TO 99.5 °F
EAR	96.4 °F TO 100.4 °F

DATE	TEMPERATURE	NOTES

DOCTOR'S APPOINTMENT

DATE	DOCTOR	REASON / DIAGNOSIS	MEDICATION

MEDICINE TRACKING

MEDICATION NAME:

DOSAGE: TIMES PER DAY:

DATE	TIME GIVEN	NEXT DUE	REMARKS

ADDITIONAL NOTES

FEEDING SCHEDULE

DATE:

TIME	DURATION (BREASTFEEDING)	AMOUNT (BOTTLE)	NOTES

DIAPER

TIME	PEE	POOP

NAP TIME

START TIME	WAKEUP TIME	TOTAL MINUTES/ HOURS

FOOD

TIME	FOOD	AMOUNT

NOTES & REMINDERS

BABY'S TEMPERATURE

METHOD	RANGE
RECTUM	97.9 °F TO 100.4 °F
MOUTH	95.9 °F TO 99.5 °F
ARMPIT	97.8 °F TO 99.5 °F
EAR	96.4 °F TO 100.4 °F

DATE	TEMPERATURE	NOTES

DOCTOR'S APPOINTMENT

DATE	DOCTOR	REASON / DIAGNOSIS	MEDICATION

MEDICINE TRACKING

MEDICATION NAME:

DOSAGE: TIMES PER DAY:

DATE	TIME GIVEN	NEXT DUE	REMARKS

ADDITIONAL NOTES

FEEDING SCHEDULE

DATE:

TIME	DURATION (BREASTFEEDING)	AMOUNT (BOTTLE)	NOTES

DIAPER

TIME	PEE	POOP

NAP TIME

START TIME	WAKEUP TIME	TOTAL MINUTES/ HOURS

FOOD

TIME	FOOD	AMOUNT

NOTES & REMINDERS

BABY'S TEMPERATURE

METHOD	RANGE
RECTUM	97.9 °F TO 100.4 °F
MOUTH	95.9 °F TO 99.5 °F
ARMPIT	97.8 °F TO 99.5 °F
EAR	96.4 °F TO 100.4 °F

DATE	TEMPERATURE	NOTES

DOCTOR'S APPOINTMENT

DATE	DOCTOR	REASON / DIAGNOSIS	MEDICATION

MEDICINE TRACKING

MEDICATION NAME:

DOSAGE: TIMES PER DAY:

DATE	TIME GIVEN	NEXT DUE	REMARKS

ADDITIONAL NOTES

FEEDING SCHEDULE

DATE:

TIME	DURATION (BREASTFEEDING)	AMOUNT (BOTTLE)	NOTES

DIAPER

TIME	PEE	POOP

NAP TIME

START TIME	WAKEUP TIME	TOTAL MINUTES/ HOURS

FOOD

TIME	FOOD	AMOUNT

NOTES & REMINDERS

BABY'S TEMPERATURE

METHOD	RANGE
RECTUM	97.9 °F TO 100.4 °F
MOUTH	95.9 °F TO 99.5 °F
ARMPIT	97.8 °F TO 99.5 °F
EAR	96.4 °F TO 100.4 °F

DATE	TEMPERATURE	NOTES

DOCTOR'S APPOINTMENT

DATE	DOCTOR	REASON / DIAGNOSIS	MEDICATION

MEDICINE TRACKING

MEDICATION NAME:

DOSAGE: TIMES PER DAY:

DATE	TIME GIVEN	NEXT DUE	REMARKS

ADDITIONAL NOTES

FEEDING SCHEDULE

DATE:

TIME	DURATION (BREASTFEEDING)	AMOUNT (BOTTLE)	NOTES

DIAPER

TIME	PEE	POOP

NAP TIME

START TIME	WAKEUP TIME	TOTAL MINUTES/ HOURS

FOOD

TIME	FOOD	AMOUNT

NOTES & REMINDERS

BABY'S TEMPERATURE

METHOD	RANGE
RECTUM	97.9 °F TO 100.4 °F
MOUTH	95.9 °F TO 99.5 °F
ARMPIT	97.8 °F TO 99.5 °F
EAR	96.4 °F TO 100.4 °F

DATE	TEMPERATURE	NOTES

DOCTOR'S APPOINTMENT

DATE	DOCTOR	REASON / DIAGNOSIS	MEDICATION

MEDICINE TRACKING

MEDICATION NAME:

DOSAGE: TIMES PER DAY:

DATE	TIME GIVEN	NEXT DUE	REMARKS

ADDITIONAL NOTES

FEEDING SCHEDULE

DATE:

TIME	DURATION (BREASTFEEDING)	AMOUNT (BOTTLE)	NOTES

DIAPER

TIME	PEE	POOP

NAP TIME

START TIME	WAKEUP TIME	TOTAL MINUTES/ HOURS

FOOD

TIME	FOOD	AMOUNT

NOTES & REMINDERS

BABY'S TEMPERATURE

METHOD	RANGE
RECTUM	97.9 °F TO 100.4 °F
MOUTH	95.9 °F TO 99.5 °F
ARMPIT	97.8 °F TO 99.5 °F
EAR	96.4 °F TO 100.4 °F

DATE	TEMPERATURE	NOTES

DOCTOR'S APPOINTMENT

DATE	DOCTOR	REASON / DIAGNOSIS	MEDICATION

MEDICINE TRACKING

MEDICATION NAME:

DOSAGE: TIMES PER DAY:

DATE	TIME GIVEN	NEXT DUE	REMARKS

ADDITIONAL NOTES

FEEDING SCHEDULE

DATE:

TIME	DURATION (BREASTFEEDING)	AMOUNT (BOTTLE)	NOTES

DIAPER

TIME	PEE	POOP

NAP TIME

START TIME	WAKEUP TIME	TOTAL MINUTES/ HOURS

FOOD

TIME	FOOD	AMOUNT

NOTES & REMINDERS

BABY'S TEMPERATURE

METHOD	RANGE
RECTUM	97.9 °F TO 100.4 °F
MOUTH	95.9 °F TO 99.5 °F
ARMPIT	97.8 °F TO 99.5 °F
EAR	96.4 °F TO 100.4 °F

DATE	TEMPERATURE	NOTES

DOCTOR'S APPOINTMENT

DATE	DOCTOR	REASON / DIAGNOSIS	MEDICATION

MEDICINE TRACKING

MEDICATION NAME:

DOSAGE: TIMES PER DAY:

DATE	TIME GIVEN	NEXT DUE	REMARKS

ADDITIONAL NOTES

FEEDING SCHEDULE

DATE:

TIME	DURATION (BREASTFEEDING)	AMOUNT (BOTTLE)	NOTES

DIAPER

TIME	PEE	POOP

NAP TIME

START TIME	WAKEUP TIME	TOTAL MINUTES/ HOURS

FOOD

TIME	FOOD	AMOUNT

NOTES & REMINDERS

BABY'S TEMPERATURE

METHOD	RANGE
RECTUM	97.9 °F TO 100.4 °F
MOUTH	95.9 °F TO 99.5 °F
ARMPIT	97.8 °F TO 99.5 °F
EAR	96.4 °F TO 100.4 °F

DATE	TEMPERATURE	NOTES

DOCTOR'S APPOINTMENT

DATE	DOCTOR	REASON / DIAGNOSIS	MEDICATION

MEDICINE TRACKING

MEDICATION NAME:

DOSAGE: TIMES PER DAY:

DATE	TIME GIVEN	NEXT DUE	REMARKS

ADDITIONAL NOTES

FEEDING SCHEDULE

DATE:

TIME	DURATION (BREASTFEEDING)	AMOUNT (BOTTLE)	NOTES

DIAPER

TIME	PEE	POOP

NAP TIME

START TIME	WAKEUP TIME	TOTAL MINUTES/ HOURS

FOOD

TIME	FOOD	AMOUNT

NOTES & REMINDERS

BABY'S TEMPERATURE

METHOD	RANGE
RECTUM	97.9 °F TO 100.4 °F
MOUTH	95.9 °F TO 99.5 °F
ARMPIT	97.8 °F TO 99.5 °F
EAR	96.4 °F TO 100.4 °F

DATE	TEMPERATURE	NOTES

DOCTOR'S APPOINTMENT

DATE	DOCTOR	REASON / DIAGNOSIS	MEDICATION

MEDICINE TRACKING

MEDICATION NAME:

DOSAGE: TIMES PER DAY:

DATE	TIME GIVEN	NEXT DUE	REMARKS

ADDITIONAL NOTES

FEEDING SCHEDULE

DATE:

TIME	DURATION (BREASTFEEDING)	AMOUNT (BOTTLE)	NOTES

DIAPER

TIME	PEE	POOP

NAP TIME

START TIME	WAKEUP TIME	TOTAL MINUTES/ HOURS

FOOD

TIME	FOOD	AMOUNT

NOTES & REMINDERS

BABY'S TEMPERATURE

METHOD	RANGE
RECTUM	97.9 °F TO 100.4 °F
MOUTH	95.9 °F TO 99.5 °F
ARMPIT	97.8 °F TO 99.5 °F
EAR	96.4 °F TO 100.4 °F

DATE	TEMPERATURE	NOTES

DOCTOR'S APPOINTMENT

DATE	DOCTOR	REASON / DIAGNOSIS	MEDICATION

MEDICINE TRACKING

MEDICATION NAME:

DOSAGE: TIMES PER DAY:

DATE	TIME GIVEN	NEXT DUE	REMARKS

ADDITIONAL NOTES

FEEDING SCHEDULE

DATE:

TIME	DURATION (BREASTFEEDING)	AMOUNT (BOTTLE)	NOTES

DIAPER

TIME	PEE	POOP

NAP TIME

START TIME	WAKEUP TIME	TOTAL MINUTES/ HOURS

FOOD

TIME	FOOD	AMOUNT

NOTES & REMINDERS

BABY'S TEMPERATURE

METHOD	RANGE
RECTUM	97.9 °F TO 100.4 °F
MOUTH	95.9 °F TO 99.5 °F
ARMPIT	97.8 °F TO 99.5 °F
EAR	96.4 °F TO 100.4 °F

DATE	TEMPERATURE	NOTES

DOCTOR'S APPOINTMENT

DATE	DOCTOR	REASON / DIAGNOSIS	MEDICATION

MEDICINE TRACKING

MEDICATION NAME:

DOSAGE: TIMES PER DAY:

DATE	TIME GIVEN	NEXT DUE	REMARKS

ADDITIONAL NOTES

FEEDING SCHEDULE

DATE:

TIME	DURATION (BREASTFEEDING)	AMOUNT (BOTTLE)	NOTES

DIAPER

TIME	PEE	POOP

NAP TIME

START TIME	WAKEUP TIME	TOTAL MINUTES/ HOURS

FOOD

TIME	FOOD	AMOUNT

NOTES & REMINDERS

BABY'S TEMPERATURE

METHOD	RANGE
RECTUM	97.9 °F TO 100.4 °F
MOUTH	95.9 °F TO 99.5 °F
ARMPIT	97.8 °F TO 99.5 °F
EAR	96.4 °F TO 100.4 °F

DATE	TEMPERATURE	NOTES

DOCTOR'S APPOINTMENT

DATE	DOCTOR	REASON / DIAGNOSIS	MEDICATION

MEDICINE TRACKING

MEDICATION NAME:

DOSAGE: TIMES PER DAY:

DATE	TIME GIVEN	NEXT DUE	REMARKS

ADDITIONAL NOTES

FEEDING SCHEDULE

DATE:

TIME	DURATION (BREASTFEEDING)	AMOUNT (BOTTLE)	NOTES

DIAPER

TIME	PEE	POOP

NAP TIME

START TIME	WAKEUP TIME	TOTAL MINUTES/ HOURS

FOOD

TIME	FOOD	AMOUNT

NOTES & REMINDERS

BABY'S TEMPERATURE

METHOD	RANGE
RECTUM	97.9 °F TO 100.4 °F
MOUTH	95.9 °F TO 99.5 °F
ARMPIT	97.8 °F TO 99.5 °F
EAR	96.4 °F TO 100.4 °F

DATE	TEMPERATURE	NOTES

DOCTOR'S APPOINTMENT

DATE	DOCTOR	REASON / DIAGNOSIS	MEDICATION

MEDICINE TRACKING

MEDICATION NAME:

DOSAGE: TIMES PER DAY:

DATE	TIME GIVEN	NEXT DUE	REMARKS

ADDITIONAL NOTES

FEEDING SCHEDULE

DATE:

TIME	DURATION (BREASTFEEDING)	AMOUNT (BOTTLE)	NOTES

DIAPER

TIME	PEE	POOP

NAP TIME

START TIME	WAKEUP TIME	TOTAL MINUTES/ HOURS

FOOD

TIME	FOOD	AMOUNT

NOTES & REMINDERS

BABY'S TEMPERATURE

METHOD	RANGE
RECTUM	97.9 °F TO 100.4 °F
MOUTH	95.9 °F TO 99.5 °F
ARMPIT	97.8 °F TO 99.5 °F
EAR	96.4 °F TO 100.4 °F

DATE	TEMPERATURE	NOTES

DOCTOR'S APPOINTMENT

DATE	DOCTOR	REASON / DIAGNOSIS	MEDICATION

MEDICINE TRACKING

MEDICATION NAME:

DOSAGE: TIMES PER DAY:

DATE	TIME GIVEN	NEXT DUE	REMARKS

ADDITIONAL NOTES

FEEDING SCHEDULE

DATE:

TIME	DURATION (BREASTFEEDING)	AMOUNT (BOTTLE)	NOTES

DIAPER

TIME	PEE	POOP

NAP TIME

START TIME	WAKEUP TIME	TOTAL MINUTES/ HOURS

FOOD

TIME	FOOD	AMOUNT

NOTES & REMINDERS

BABY'S TEMPERATURE

METHOD	RANGE
RECTUM	97.9 °F TO 100.4 °F
MOUTH	95.9 °F TO 99.5 °F
ARMPIT	97.8 °F TO 99.5 °F
EAR	96.4 °F TO 100.4 °F

DATE	TEMPERATURE	NOTES

DOCTOR'S APPOINTMENT

DATE	DOCTOR	REASON / DIAGNOSIS	MEDICATION

MEDICINE TRACKING

MEDICATION NAME:

DOSAGE: TIMES PER DAY:

DATE	TIME GIVEN	NEXT DUE	REMARKS

ADDITIONAL NOTES

FEEDING SCHEDULE

DATE:

TIME	DURATION (BREASTFEEDING)	AMOUNT (BOTTLE)	NOTES

DIAPER

TIME	PEE	POOP

NAP TIME

START TIME	WAKEUP TIME	TOTAL MINUTES/ HOURS

FOOD

TIME	FOOD	AMOUNT

NOTES & REMINDERS

BABY'S TEMPERATURE

METHOD	RANGE
RECTUM	97.9 °F TO 100.4 °F
MOUTH	95.9 °F TO 99.5 °F
ARMPIT	97.8 °F TO 99.5 °F
EAR	96.4 °F TO 100.4 °F

DATE	TEMPERATURE	NOTES

DOCTOR'S APPOINTMENT

DATE	DOCTOR	REASON / DIAGNOSIS	MEDICATION

MEDICINE TRACKING

MEDICATION NAME:

DOSAGE: TIMES PER DAY:

DATE	TIME GIVEN	NEXT DUE	REMARKS

ADDITIONAL NOTES

FEEDING SCHEDULE

DATE:

TIME	DURATION (BREASTFEEDING)	AMOUNT (BOTTLE)	NOTES

DIAPER

TIME	PEE	POOP

NAP TIME

START TIME	WAKEUP TIME	TOTAL MINUTES/ HOURS

FOOD

TIME	FOOD	AMOUNT

NOTES & REMINDERS

BABY'S TEMPERATURE

METHOD	RANGE
RECTUM	97.9 °F TO 100.4 °F
MOUTH	95.9 °F TO 99.5 °F
ARMPIT	97.8 °F TO 99.5 °F
EAR	96.4 °F TO 100.4 °F

DATE	TEMPERATURE	NOTES

DOCTOR'S APPOINTMENT

DATE	DOCTOR	REASON / DIAGNOSIS	MEDICATION

MEDICINE TRACKING

MEDICATION NAME:

DOSAGE: TIMES PER DAY:

DATE	TIME GIVEN	NEXT DUE	REMARKS

ADDITIONAL NOTES

FEEDING SCHEDULE

DATE:

TIME	DURATION (BREASTFEEDING)	AMOUNT (BOTTLE)	NOTES

DIAPER

TIME	PEE	POOP

NAP TIME

START TIME	WAKEUP TIME	TOTAL MINUTES/ HOURS

FOOD

TIME	FOOD	AMOUNT

NOTES & REMINDERS

BABY'S TEMPERATURE

METHOD	RANGE
RECTUM	97.9 °F TO 100.4 °F
MOUTH	95.9 °F TO 99.5 °F
ARMPIT	97.8 °F TO 99.5 °F
EAR	96.4 °F TO 100.4 °F

DATE	TEMPERATURE	NOTES

DOCTOR'S APPOINTMENT

DATE	DOCTOR	REASON / DIAGNOSIS	MEDICATION

MEDICINE TRACKING

MEDICATION NAME:

DOSAGE: TIMES PER DAY:

DATE	TIME GIVEN	NEXT DUE	REMARKS

ADDITIONAL NOTES

FEEDING SCHEDULE

DATE:

TIME	DURATION (BREASTFEEDING)	AMOUNT (BOTTLE)	NOTES

DIAPER

TIME	PEE	POOP

NAP TIME

START TIME	WAKEUP TIME	TOTAL MINUTES/ HOURS

FOOD

TIME	FOOD	AMOUNT

NOTES & REMINDERS

BABY'S TEMPERATURE

METHOD	RANGE
RECTUM	97.9 °F TO 100.4 °F
MOUTH	95.9 °F TO 99.5 °F
ARMPIT	97.8 °F TO 99.5 °F
EAR	96.4 °F TO 100.4 °F

DATE	TEMPERATURE	NOTES

DOCTOR'S APPOINTMENT

DATE	DOCTOR	REASON / DIAGNOSIS	MEDICATION

MEDICINE TRACKING

MEDICATION NAME:

DOSAGE: TIMES PER DAY:

DATE	TIME GIVEN	NEXT DUE	REMARKS

ADDITIONAL NOTES

www.ingramcontent.com/pod-product-compliance
Lightning Source LLC
Chambersburg PA
CBHW081229080526
44587CB00022B/3877